sundance
LITTLE BLUE
R E A D E R S

What If...?

Focus: Designing, Making and Appraising
Materials
Systems

PETER SLOAN &
SHERYL SLOAN

What would it be like if there were no telephones? We would not be able to talk to friends far away. We would need to write lots of letters.

What would it be like if there was no television? We would read more books and play more games with our family.

What would it be like if
there were no cars?
We would walk to school.
We would not go as far
from home or be able to
get around as much.

What would it be like if there were no airplanes? People would not be able to fly to other countries. Crossing an ocean by boat could take months.

What would it be like if there were no washing machines? People would have to wash clothes by hand.

What would it be like if there were no refrigerators? We would not be able to have cold drinks or eat ice cream.

What would it be like if there was no electricity? We would not have any lights, radios, or computers. Think of all the things that use electricity. They would not be there.